Self-Direction

Taking Positive Risks, Following Your Dreams

by Robert Wandberg, PhD

Consultants:
Roberta Brack Kaufman, EdD
Dean, College of Education
Concordia University
St. Paul, Minnesota

Millie Shepich, MPH, CHES
Health Educator and District Health Coordinator
Waubonsie Valley High School
Aurora, Illinois

LifeMatters
an imprint of Capstone Press
Mankato, Minnesota

Thank you to Heather Thomson of BRAVO Middle School, Bloomington, Minnesota; to Christine Ramsay of Kennedy High School, Bloomington, Minnesota; and especially to all of their students, who developed the self-assessments and provided lots of real stories.

LifeMatters Books are published by Capstone Press
PO Box 669 • 151 Good Counsel Drive • Mankato, Minnesota 56002
http://www.capstone-press.com

Printed in the United States of America

Library of Congress Cataloging-in-Publication Data
Wandberg, Robert.
     Self-Direction: taking positive risks, following your dreams / by Robert Wandberg.
         p.   cm. — (Life skills)
     Includes bibliographical references and index.
     Summary: Discusses ways that young people can aquire self-knowledge, balance their physical, mental, and emotional sides, make good and healthy choices, pursue their dreams, and share themselves with the community.
     ISBN 0-7368-0696-2 (hardcover) — ISBN 0-7368-8837-3 (softcover)
     1. Autonomy in adolescence—Juvenile literature. 2. Self-management (Psychology) for teenagers—Juvenile literature. [1. Conduct of life. 2. Self-perception.] I. Title.
     BF724.3.A88 W36 2000
     158.1´0835—dc21
                                          00-022518
                                          CIP

Staff Credits
Charles Pederson, editor; Adam Lazar, designer; Katy Kudela, photo researcher

Photo Credits
Cover: UPmagazine/©Tim Yoon
Emotion/©Artville, 16; 26; ©Stockbyte, 31
FPG/©Danilo Nardi Photography, 39
Index Stock Imagery/9
International Stock/©Clint Clemens, 37; ©James Davis, 59
Photo Network/©Mary Messenger, 17; Tom McCarthy Photos, 28
Unicorn Stock Photos/©Tom McCarthy, 10; ©Eric R. Berndt, 12; ©Aneal Vohra, 20; ©Jim Shippee, 34; ©A. Gurmankin, 38; ©James L. Fly, 53; ©Martha McBride, 55
UPmagazine/©Tim Yoon, 5, 15, 23, 33, 43, 51
Visuals Unlimited/©Jeff Greenberg, 49

A 0 9 8 7 6 5 4 3 2 1

Table of Contents

Chapter **Overview**

People who are self-directed can make their own decisions. They feel confident to stand by what they want even when pressured to do otherwise.

Self-assessments can give us information to understand ourselves better.

All behavior has consequences.

Teens behave in ways that can deeply affect their health now and in the future.

CHAPTER 1

Know Yourself, Know Your Choices

What Is Self-Direction?

This book is about self-direction. That's a state of being confident and respecting the health and safety of you and other people.

Being self-directed often involves setting short-term and long-term goals. Self-directed people are usually optimistic, keeping a hopeful, positive, and cheerful attitude. When problems arise, people who are self-directed often see possibilities rather than impossible obstacles. People who are self-directed often take positive risks and follow their instincts. They do so even when others pressure them to do something else. This self-confidence is called individualism.

Healthy, confident people are usually self-directed. They are involved in **KnowingMatters.** What they know and how they know it shape their attitudes and behaviors. In this chapter you will learn the characteristics of a self-directed person. You also will take a self-assessment that can help you predict risks and set goals.

QUOTE

"To thine own self be true." –William Shakespeare

Kim, Age 15

Kim was on her school's debate team. She always dreamed of doing well in the debate championship and becoming a famous speaker. However, her grades were falling because she practiced so much. Her coach said Kim needed at least a C average to stay on the team. Kim was miserable, but she decided it was up to her whether she competed. To reach her dream, she would need a lot of extra effort. She was determined to study harder, bring her grades up, and win the debate championship. She went to ask the school counselor if any students could tutor her.

Self-Direction

"You always see those self-tests in magazines. You know what I mean. 'Are you in love?' 'What's your fashion sense?' They're usually pretty dumb. However, sometimes they can help you learn about yourself."
−Robert, age 16

Self-Assessments

Self-assessments are tests that can give us information to help us know ourselves better. There are many kinds of self-assessments. Teen self-assessments often are about relationships or health risks and attitudes. Common topics include risk of heart disease, cancer, or mental illness. Other topics may include attitudes about the death penalty or about abortion, which ends a pregnancy early. Schools may provide self-assessments to help students predict success in career choices.

By periodically assessing yourself, you can keep track of what is normal for you. The key to self-assessments is that *you* interpret the information, not someone else.

Try the following self-assessment. It can help you identify self-directed behaviors you may want to work on. Everyone is self-directed at least some of the time. With practice, most people can become more confident about the decisions that guide their personal behavior.

How Self-Directed Am I?

Read items 1–15. On a separate sheet of paper, write the number that best describes you. Use this rating scale:

Always = 3	Sometimes = 2	Never = 1

1. I have good critical thinking skills. I examine and use information in my life.	3	2	1
2. I decide for myself.	3	2	1
3. I have a plan for my education.	3	2	1
4. I want to get a good-paying job.	3	2	1
5. I know what career I want when I am an adult.	3	2	1
6. I have a plan for my life besides working.	3	2	1
7. I have long-term goals and dreams for my life.	3	2	1

Self-Direction

8. I can achieve my goals and dreams.   **3**   **2**   **1**

9. I make good choices for my life.   **3**   **2**   **1**

10. My health habits help me achieve my goals.   **3**   **2**   **1**

11. I consider what might happen as a result of
    my decisions.   **3**   **2**   **1**

12. I am up to any challenge I face.   **3**   **2**   **1**

13. I know the difference between right and
    wrong.   **3**   **2**   **1**

14. I have a strong knowledge of health and how
    to stay healthy.   **3**   **2**   **1**

15. I can apply my health knowledge to my life.   **3**   **2**   **1**

Add up your points. According to the teens who developed this
self-assessment, you want to score close to 45. The closer you are
to 45, the more self-directed you probably are. For items you scored
1 or 2 on, it probably means you need more practice or thought.

Consequences and Options

Your health decisions and behaviors have consequences. Many people think of consequences as being only bad. That's true sometimes. However, consequences can be positive. For example, teens who practice a hobby or skill often receive the positive consequence of being recognized. A positive consequence of hard work at school is graduation. Good friendships are a positive consequence of kind and outgoing behavior.

Most people, including teens, have goals for their life. Health can affect your goals such as traveling, getting a job, or having children. If teens aren't healthy, it's hard to accomplish their life goals. Teens can decide to eat well, exercise, and avoid tobacco, alcohol, and other drugs. They can choose to be optimistic. These teens have a high likelihood of achieving their goals.

Teen pregnancy rates are higher in the United States than in many other industrial countries. U.S. rates are almost twice as high as in Canada, England, or Wales. They are nine times higher than in Japan.

On the other hand, teens who choose high-risk health behaviors are less likely to reach life goals. Their behaviors can have consequences that are minor and last only a short time. However, some health consequences can be serious and last for a long time. For example, a person may catch a serious disease that can be spread during sexual contact. This is called a sexually transmitted disease (STD) or sexually transmitted infection (STI). Some kinds of STDs can make a person physically unable to have children. Some are deadly.

Your Choices Matter

How might health consequences affect a person's goals? As an example, consider a teen who wanted to be a professional violin player. By using alcohol or other drugs, that teen might not be able to practice because of a hangover. That teen might have a car crash that hinders his or her ability to play. The teen might even be killed in an accident, ending that goal forever.

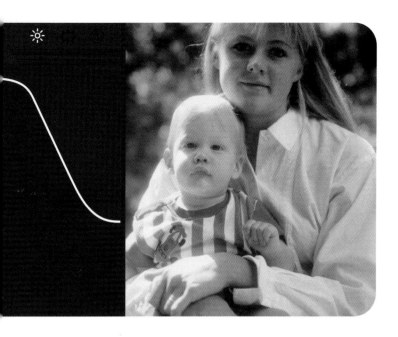

As another example, nearly a million teen girls become pregnant each year in the United States. Most teen pregnancies are unplanned. Teen pregnancy can affect the future of the mother, father, and child. The teen couple has to decide what action to take about the pregnancy. Most teen mothers raise the child alone without the father's help.

Many teen mothers drop out of school to take care of the baby. Children are expensive to care for, and parents are responsible for them for many years. Relationships between the mother and father may become strained when there's an unplanned pregnancy. All of these consequences can change the teens' goals or make them unreachable.

"I can't believe how much having a baby changed my life. Everything is hard. I barely ever see my friends. My college plans are put off for I don't know how long. Maybe forever. My advice is either don't have sex until you're ready for a baby, or else use good birth control."—Lee, age 18

By knowing ourself and our choices, we can begin to make better health decisions. Even if we already make good health choices, there's always room for improvement.

Points to Consider: KnowingMatters

Do you think it's important not to give up on your goals? Why or why not?

How can taking a health assessment today help you plan for the future? Explain.

How do you think self-direction is related to your health?

What areas of your life would you like to improve? Explain.

Chapter **Overview**

Health can be defined in many ways. It can mean completely different things depending on the time, place, or person.

Three major areas of health involve physical, mental or emotional, and social health. You can think of these areas as three interlocking circles.

Knowledge is power. Living a healthy life depends on practicing healthy habits.

CHAPTER 2

A Picture of Health

Everyone wants to be healthy. However, it's not always easy to make healthy choices. This chapter will help you learn what it means to be healthy. These **HealthMatters** involve looking at your total health.

Defining Health

Ask your friends how they would define the word *health*. They might say it's when you're not sick. A common definition of health is more than the absence of disease or illness. It also includes complete physical, mental, and social well-being. Good health is based on more than how far a person can run, for example. It includes a positive mental attitude and strong social connections as well.

Health often means different things to different people. In one place, people may consider one type of physical appearance to be healthy. In another place, the opposite physical appearance may be the healthy look. For example, North Americans often consider thin people to be beautiful. In another part of the world, the same thin people might be considered unhealthy. The way some societies treat diseases helps to define their view of health. Singing, chanting, dancing, natural remedies, prayer, medicines, or equipment are used differently across cultures.

Even in the same culture, ideas about health may change. For example, in North America during the 1800s, many people thought that extremely pale skin was considered healthy. Today, many people view such pale skin as a sign of illness.

How does health relate to self-direction? Self-directed people usually focus on their total health. The people of ancient Greece called this focus a "sound mind in a sound body." Some experts put it this way: Health is a quality of life through which life goals and dreams may be achieved.

David, Age 17

David was a star athlete in his high school. He was in top physical shape. He was captain of three varsity teams—cross-country, basketball, and tennis. David never missed a day of practice. His coaches said David was a dedicated athlete who even practiced on his own on weekends.

David is in good physical condition. He is a faithful and committed athlete. Is David healthy? Some people might say yes. However, other people might say it's difficult to judge David's health on this information alone. To know if David is really healthy, we would need to know more about him. We would want to find out about his state of mind and his connection to other people. For example, we would want to know if he has close friends or is an upbeat person.

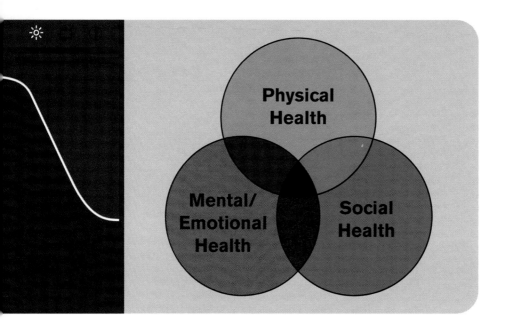

One way to look at your health is to divide it into three interlocking circles. One circle represents physical health, one represents mental and emotional health, and one represents social health.

Each circle shows a part of health. Each is closely connected to the others. The different parts of health often affect each other. For example, a physical illness or injury may make a person depressed. Depression can make it difficult to remain mentally or socially healthy. Depressed people may withdraw from their friends temporarily. Ongoing worry or stress may weaken the body's physical defenses against sickness. This can lower a person's resistance to long-lasting, chronic illnesses such as heart disease or other diseases.

Self-Direction

The Centers for Disease Control and Prevention (CDC) says any physical exercise is good for you. For example, walking rapidly for 30 minutes per day can strengthen the heart. It also can lower blood pressure and keep off extra weight.

Sam, Age 18

Sam normally was a friendly and outgoing teen with lots of friends. He usually got good grades. However, he became sick a week before a big test and couldn't study as much as he wanted. As a result, he didn't do well. He was sad and angry about the test for several days and didn't want to talk with anyone. He stayed in his room and wouldn't even speak with his girlfriend. His friends began to avoid him in the halls at school.

Physical Health

The first circle involves physical health. If you are physically healthy, you work to maintain your body's health through good nutrition and regular exercise. Getting enough sleep, and not smoking or using harmful drugs are other examples of maintaining good physical health. People who are self-directed often can choose and control these healthy behaviors. The behaviors that a person can control are sometimes called lifestyle behaviors.

Other factors in physical health are less easy to control. For example, certain illnesses such as diabetes or heart disease may occur in a person's family. These diseases may be passed to children. Another person may live in an environment that can affect health. Chapter 3 describes these health factors in more detail.

Mental and Emotional Health

Mental and emotional health make up the second circle. People with good mental and emotional health can set short-term and long-term goals. They are often hopeful and believe they can meet challenges. They are curious and interested in life and like to learn new things. They can tolerate differences and cope with change. They usually recognize and can appropriately express their emotions. They often take positive risks, think clearly, and understand and can communicate their feelings.

Values can be included in this circle, too. Values are standards or qualities that a person considers to be good or worthwhile.

Social Health

The third circle, social health, is about relationships with family, friends, teachers, and other people. People with good social health usually get along well with others. They are often aware of how they relate to their community and the larger environment. They commonly share the responsibility for improving the area in which they live.

People with good social health often have satisfying relationships with people of all ages. They can make and keep friends and are fun to be with. They often are good listeners and are willing to help other people.

Self-Direction

"My brother jogs and works out a lot. He's in great shape. However, he hardly has any friends and mostly stays in his room. He also complains about every little thing he's asked to do. I guess he's healthy in some ways but not in every way."–Eva, age 14

The Bottom Line

Here's the bottom line. You can become healthy if you practice healthy habits. Most teens have probably developed some good and some poor health habits. Stay with the good habits. Get rid of or change the poor habits.

Points to Consider: HealthMatters

What words would you use to define a healthy person? Explain.

Why do you think the United States has a higher teen pregnancy rate than many other countries?

How can one circle of health affect another? Give an example.

Which of the three circles of health do you think is hardest for teens to achieve? Why?

Chapter **Overview**

Genetics, environment, health care, and lifestyle contribute to life expectancy. Of these contributors, lifestyle choices are most related to premature death.

You are in charge of your lifestyle choices.

Your choices affect your health.

CHAPTER 3

✿

Who's in Charge?

What is important in predicting your life expectancy, or how long you expect to live? Family characteristics? Your neighborhood? The availability of health care? Choices you make? You can't control all of these factors, but you can control many of them. This chapter will help you identify important health choices to help you live longer. These choices can be called **LifestyleMatters.**

FAST FACT

According to the United Nations, a Canadian born in 1998 can expect to live 79 years. In the United States, someone born in 1998 should live an average of 77 years.

Patti, Age 17

"My uncle was a cancer specialist. You'd think a doctor like him would know better, but he smoked a lot. He said he started when he was 14. He smoked at least a pack a day, probably more. He got lung cancer when he was about 50, so they took out most of one lung. Even with one lung gone, he kept smoking. He seemed healthy before the operation, but afterward, he became like a little, old man. He ended up dying of a heart attack a couple of years later. I can't believe how young he was."

Contributors to Premature Death

Many teens can think of someone who died earlier than seemed natural. Early deaths like this are called premature deaths. Currently in North America, the average person can expect to live past age 70.

Why do people die prematurely? One way to look at premature death is to consider the contributors to a person's life expectancy. Four contributors are genetics, environment, health care, and lifestyle.

Self-Direction

Lead is the number one environmental poison facing many children in Canada and the United States. Nearly a million children ages 1 to 5 have high levels of lead in their blood. These levels put young children at risk for learning disabilities or behavior problems. If the level of lead in the blood is high enough, it can cause unconsciousness or even death. The main source of lead poisoning is lead-based house paints.

Genetics

In many ways, you are made up of characteristics that you inherit from your parents. For example, your nose may be the same shape as your mother's. You may have your father's curly hair. You even may have traits from your grandparents or great-grandparents. These inherited traits are genetic. That is, they are passed from parents to children.

Like physical traits, some diseases are genetic. You can't control whether you have genetic diseases. You simply are born with them. Some experts suggest that people also can be born with the likelihood of having certain health problems. For example, heart disease is more likely in some people than others. A person's gender also may influence health. For example, males on average have more heart attacks at a younger age when compared to females.

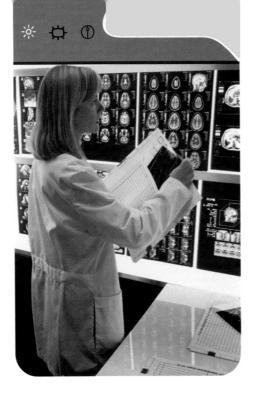

Environment

Everyone lives in a certain environment, or surroundings. An environment that includes clean air, water, and land promotes good health.

Some environments, however, can damage health. For example, some poisons in the environment, such as arsenic, are carcinogenic. They can cause cancer. Arsenic is found in substances such as certain wood preservers, insect killers, and even tobacco. Other environmental health concerns involve food, waste, water, air, and noise. Some environmental poisons such as radiation can even damage genes and cause genetic diseases in children.

Health Care

Normally, health care in North America is excellent. People can count on doctors and clinics to provide good care for health. However, mistakes do occur. As a result of health care mistakes, as many as 98,000 Americans die every year. Many people don't have enough money to visit a doctor. Without proper medical care, people are likely to become ill.

Lifestyle

Lifestyle includes the day-to-day behaviors that people choose. Lifestyle is the contributor to premature death that people can best control. The Centers for Disease Control and Prevention (CDC) notes six lifestyle areas. Poor choices in these areas contribute to most of the deaths, illness, and injury among young people. The areas are:

Tobacco use

Alcohol and other drug use

Sexual behaviors resulting in HIV infection, other STDs, or unplanned pregnancy

Eating patterns that contribute to disease

Exercise

Behaviors that result in intentional or unintentional injury. Killing oneself or others and other violent injuries are examples of intentional injuries. Car crashes, fires, and drowning are examples of unintentional injuries.

Lifestyle Challenges

Lifestyle is responsible for more premature deaths in the United States than genetics, environment, or health care systems. Consider all the behaviors and choices related to your health. It's easy to see how lifestyle can contribute to premature death.

People who are self-directed usually have and seek health knowledge. They often use that knowledge to make good health choices. These choices also can promote the health and well-being of family, friends, and their community.

People can choose healthy or unhealthy behaviors. For example, people may choose to wear a helmet or not to wear one when riding a bike. However, in an accident, a rider without a helmet is much more likely to have a permanent head injury. Consider these other examples of the way lifestyle choices can affect people's health.

Self-Direction

Chlamydia is a common STD. Its symptoms include fluid leaking from the sex organs and burning during urination. Women may experience pain below their stomach. Men may have painful or swollen testicles. Often, however, the disease has no signs.

In the United States, the STD chlamydia infects as many as 4 million people each year. It can cause females not to be able to have children. It can cause eye diseases or pneumonia in infants whose mothers have the disease. This and other STDs can be prevented by abstinence, or avoiding sexual activity. STDs also can be reduced by proper and consistent use of condoms.

An estimated 900,000 people in the United States are infected with HIV. AIDS is the leading cause of death among men age 25 to 44. Nearly 2,000 infants are born each year infected with HIV.

Every day, about 3,000 young people start smoking. Smoking-related diseases kill more than 400,000 people each year. Of people who continue to smoke regularly, about 50 percent eventually will die from smoking-related illnesses. Yet tobacco use is the most preventable cause of death. Tobacco use includes smokeless tobacco, or chew, which can cause throat disease and mouth cancer.

Diseases of the heart kill more than 700,000 people per year. These diseases often are associated with behavior such as smoking, poor diet, or lack of exercise.

We can meet these and other lifestyle challenges by paying attention to our choices. This is one way to begin to take control of our life and health.

Points to Consider: LifestyleMatters

What health habits picked up during the teen years do you think
might lead to premature death?

In your opinion, what can be done to reduce the number of premature
deaths?

Many things affect your health. What are some factors over which
you have no control?

What is the most common lifestyle challenge among teens you know?
How do you think that challenge could be overcome?

Chapter **Overview**

Self-directed people are not guaranteed an easy life.

People who are self-directed experience both failure and success. Being unsuccessful at something doesn't mean a person isn't self-directed.

There are many examples of well-known people who overcame the odds. Their self-direction helped them to succeed.

Self-Direction

CHAPTER 4

Success and Failure: A Matter of Perspective

The difference between hope and hopelessness is attitude. It may be called **TryingMatters.** Self-directed people commonly have a positive attitude. They usually keep trying to reach their dreams, despite high odds against them. Self-directed people might define failure as a nonattempt rather than a nonsuccess. Giving up or not trying at all is worse than trying and not succeeding.

In this chapter you will read the stories of people who didn't give up. They include Marian Anderson, Thomas Edison, Babe Ruth, and George Washington Carver. Other examples are Muhammad Ali, Oprah Winfrey, Gloria Estefan, and Tom Cruise.

Tensions were building between longtime students and new students from Vietnam. Jay and his friends wanted the immigrants out. Finally, a teacher offered students extra credit for meeting with him and some of the immigrants. Jay decided to go. "It seemed like an easy way to get a better grade. But what I realized was that they were kids too, like any of us."

Jay came to believe he was wrong, so he started a group to help students understand each other. Lots of Jay's friends called him a traitor. They wouldn't talk with him anymore. Jay refused to quit. "I know that these kids aren't going away. How we get along will have a big effect on our future."

Self-Direction

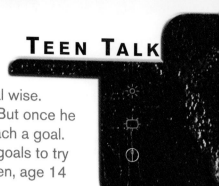

"My older brother thinks he's real wise. Usually, he just talks nonsense. But once he said, 'It's not bad if you don't reach a goal. The bad thing is not having any goals to try for.' That sounds right to me."—Ben, age 14

Examples of Self-Directed People

Being self-directed is no promise that a person will have immediate success. Actually, in some cases, the opposite may be true. Self-directed people often rely on their own judgment, which sometimes conflicts with society's accepted ideas. People who are self-directed sometimes have to overcome great odds to find success in their chosen area.

You might be able to think of famous people who went from self-direction to self-destruction. For example, Howard Hughes was one of the richest men in the world. He was active in the movie industry. His engineering firm developed important products and processes for airplanes. Yet, he died with no friends. Darryl Strawberry was an extremely talented baseball player. Yet his addiction to cocaine resulted in being suspended from major league baseball several times.

These people may have performed at their peak. However, they couldn't manage the stress of such a demanding existence.

Everyone may succeed at some things in life and not at others. Some people are good in reading, sports, mathematics, dance, art, or music. Some are good at listening and caring.

As you read, decide whether the people in this chapter had to overcome their own poor choices. Did they have to stand up for themselves against other people's ideas? Were they successes or failures? As this chapter's examples show, no one who keeps trying is a failure.

Marian Anderson

Marian Anderson was a famous African American opera singer of the 1930s and 1940s. Her first application to a music school was rejected because of her race. Still, she won several important singing competitions when she was young. As an adult, Anderson toured Europe, sang for President Franklin Roosevelt, and performed at Carnegie Hall.

At one time, Anderson wanted to perform in Washington, D.C. However, the Daughters of the American Revolution (DAR) denied her request because she was black. Instead Anderson held an outdoor concert at the Lincoln Memorial for 75,000 people. Millions more listened on the radio. Four years later the DAR invited Anderson to sing. She accepted.

Thomas Edison

Thomas Edison conducted nearly 500 experiments that failed. Finally, he perfected the light bulb.

Babe Ruth

During his baseball career, George Herman Ruth hit more home runs than any other player. Yet, he struck out more often than most other players. He still is considered one of the greatest players of all time.

George Washington Carver

George Washington Carver was born a slave in the 1860s. After gaining his freedom, he worked at many jobs until he could enter college. There he became an agricultural scientist. He was especially famous for his research with peanuts. Carver created more than 300 products from peanuts. These included a milk substitute, face powder, ink, and soap. Carver also wanted to help people of African descent. He worked to improve relations between African American and white people.

Self-Direction

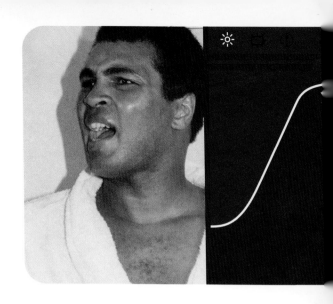

Muhammad Ali

Muhammad Ali won a gold medal in boxing at the Rome Olympics in 1960. Despite that, many people believed he was a poor boxer. Many people also disliked his personal life. He became a Muslim and gave up his birth name of Cassius Clay. This angered many people. However, he became the U.S. boxing champion in 1964 by defeating Sonny Liston.

In the late 1960s, Ali refused to enter the army to fight in Vietnam. The U.S. government put him on trial for draft dodging. The boxing commission took away his license to box. After more than three years, the U.S. Supreme Court ruled that Ali should be allowed to box again. Eventually, Ali won back the boxing title and held it for many years.

Oprah Winfrey

Oprah Winfrey had a troubled childhood. She lived with her grandmother until age 6. Then she moved in with her mother. During that time, several male relatives sexually abused her. Finally, she went to live with her father. He was strict but provided her with the discipline she needed.

Today, Winfrey is one of the most successful television hosts and producers in history. She is well on her way to becoming the United States' first African American billionaire. She shares her wealth with several charities. She has been active in getting Congress to pass laws that protect children from abuse.

QUOTE

Gloria Estefan

Gloria Estefan was born in 1957 in Havana, Cuba. Her family fled Cuba when Fidel Castro took over. Her father developed a deadly muscle disease while Estefan was still a girl. As the oldest child, she had to care for her father while her mother worked. During that time, she began to play the guitar and sing. After college, she joined a band. After years of being unknown, the band had a hit song and became extremely popular.

In 1990, a bus accident seriously injured Estefan. Her back was broken in several places, and doctors had to place metal rods in her backbone. The doctors were not optimistic that she would recover fully. However, with strength of character and support from other people, Estefan came back within a year. She immediately announced she would go on tour again. Estefan today has sold more than 45 million records.

Tom Cruise

When Tom Cruise was a child, his father moved the family many times looking for work. Cruise was a good wrestler but a poor student. He had a problem learning to read. Because he changed schools so often, he did poorly in his studies. Then he injured his knee, which ended his dream of becoming a professional wrestler. He dropped out of high school to try acting in New York City. He failed many times to get roles he wanted. Directors thought he was too intense and "not pretty enough." Finally he broke into movies and became a highly successful actor.

Points to Consider: TryingMatters

Which do you think is more common in teens, nonattempt or nonsuccess? Why?

How might success be related to attitude?

How long should a person keep trying before giving up? Explain.

How can a person balance success and failure? Do you think a person can be too self-directed?

Chapter **Overview**

A self-assessment can help you determine how many traits of self-direction you have.

Self-directed people often understand that planning for the future takes knowledge, skills, and a positive attitude.

People who are self-directed can take charge of their future.

CHAPTER 5

Take Charge

What have you done to become more self-directed? How will you strengthen your future self-direction? You can answer these questions if you know how self-directed you are. In this chapter you will learn how many traits of self-direction you have. Having these traits is helpful in preparing for **FutureMatters.**

The following self-assessment explores traits that many self-directed people possess. It can help you see how many of these traits you possess.

How Many Self-Direction Traits Do I Have?

For items 1–17, write on a piece of paper the score that best describes you: 4 = Most frequently; 3 = Very often; 2 = Sometimes; 1 = Not often.

1. **Optimism.** People who are self-directed are often optimistic. They usually are hopeful, positive, and cheerful. **4 3 2 1**

2. **Sense of humor.** People who are self-directed often can laugh and enjoy life's ups and downs. A sense of humor helps people cope better with problems large or small. Some experts believe that people with a good sense of humor have better health. **4 3 2 1**

3. **Purpose in life.** Purposeful people usually can find meaning in their life. This meaning may come from many sources such as family, friends, religion, school, or volunteer work. **4 3 2 1**

4. **Assertiveness.** Assertive people often respectfully stand up for what they believe is right. They aren't aggressive. Being assertive and aggressive are two different things. Aggressive people may stand up for what they believe in. However, they are often not polite or respectful. This attitude may lead to hurt feelings. **4 3 2 1**

5. **Friendliness.** Self-directed people are usually eager to meet new people. Often, they introduce themselves instead of waiting for others to approach them. **4 3 2 1**

6. **Self-confidence.** Self-confident people usually trust their abilities. They are not afraid to try new things and often accomplish their goals. **4 3 2 1**

7. **Established goals.** People who are self-directed 4 3 2 1
often set short-term and long-term goals. Many
of their goals are challenging. Self-directed
people commonly can change their goals if they
need to.

8. **Clear values.** People who are self-directed 4 3 2 1
usually have clear, consistent values. These help
us separate right from wrong and good from bad.

9. **Literacy skills.** Self-directed people are often 4 3 2 1
literate. That is, they can read, write, and use
mathematics. Another kind of literacy is health
literacy. Health-literate people often can find and
use health information, products, and services.

10. **Social skills.** People who are self-directed 4 3 2 1
usually enjoy being with people, and other
people enjoy being with them. They are usually
polite and respectful. Good social skills include
being honest, loyal, and dependable.

11. **Communication skills.** People who are 4 3 2 1
self-directed usually know how to communicate.
Good communication is more than talking with
someone. It involves any method of sending and
receiving messages. For example, telephones,
e-mail, letters, and body language are ways to
communicate.

12. **Ability to cope with change.** Change usually   **4**   **3**   **2**   **1**
doesn't panic people who are self-directed.
Change affects everyone in different ways. For
example, changing schools might seem like the
end of the world to one student. The same change
might not bother another student at all. People
who can cope with changes are likely to stay
healthy.

13. **Resilience.** Self-directed people have resilience.   **4**   **3**   **2**   **1**
This is the ability to bounce back from extreme
hardships or disappointments. Resilience is
related to optimism. Resilient teens live with a
hopeful, positive attitude. They are involved in
their school and the community. They have an
interest in reading and learning new information.
Most resilient people have a sense of humor and
can take charge of situations.

14. **Conflict resolution skills.** People who are   **4**   **3**   **2**   **1**
self-directed often resolve their differences by
changing their own behavior, not other people's.
In conflicts, it takes maturity to look objectively
at one's behavior and change it if needed.
Healthy conflict resolution requires people to
share feelings, talk calmly, and focus on the
issues. Self-directed people often can do that.

15. **Critical thinking skills.** People who are self-directed often can think critically about information, products, and services. They ask themselves whether the information communicates ideas truthfully. They consider the evidence before deciding.

4 3 2 1

16. **Advocacy.** Self-directed people often advocate. This means they argue for a cause or speak on another person's behalf. Many teens advocate for issues, laws, or behaviors they care about deeply. They get involved in the concerns of their family and community.

4 3 2 1

17. **Responsibility.** People who are self-directed commonly accept responsibility for what they do. They usually have strong values. Responsible people may do the right thing, even under pressure to do the wrong thing. They often feel that they owe something to the health and well-being of family, friends, and community.

4 3 2 1

Add up your score. The closer it is to 68, the more self-directed you may be. Don't worry if you don't score 3 or 4 on all of these traits. Most people don't. However, lower scores can show you where you can improve.

The group Students Against Destructive Decisions (SADD) is made up of teens. They advocate for healthier teen lives. SADD groups can be found in all 50 states, all over Canada, and in other countries.

What Does It All Mean?

People who are self-directed often can take charge of their life. They commonly develop skills such as literacy, math, and critical thinking. Such skills can give them confidence to reach personal goals. Besides these lifelong skills, self-directed people may develop interests in music, the arts, or other areas. People who are self-directed often have strong interpersonal skills. These skills allow people to get along with each other.

Diann, Age 19

Diann wasn't happy with all of her behaviors. However, she was practicing in several areas where she needed work. One area she wanted to improve was her friendliness. She decided to introduce herself to one new person a week. She wanted to be more optimistic, so she was trying to look at the bright side of things. Finally, she wanted to advocate for important issues. To do that, she joined a group that worked to help her fellow students who had children. She knew she needed more practice. Still, Diann felt good about the direction her life was taking.

Points to Consider: FutureMatters

Which qualities of self-direction from the assessment do you feel are most important? Why?

Which qualities of self-direction do you feel most teens have? Why?

Which qualities of self-direction do you feel most teens don't have? Why?

How can schools help students gain self-direction qualities? Explain.

Chapter **Overview**

You can begin to share your skills and needs with a larger community. This is a step toward gaining a sense of power.

When you share ideas and skills, you begin to know that your work has paid off.

You may feel a sense of deep pride when your actions positively affect a larger community.

CHAPTER 6

Expand Yourself

You have many unique skills. Perhaps you have a sense of humor or are considerate of others. Maybe your friends have said that you are a good listener. Maybe you're a great math student. In this chapter you will learn to recognize those skills. You also will see how you can use them to help others. Expanding yourself in this way may be called **OtherMatters.**

Recognizing Your Strengths

Everyone has strengths. However, we may have learned to see only our faults. To help ourselves become more self-directed, it's helpful to know what we are good at. One good way to think about our strengths is to write a list. For example, imagine writing your name. After each letter, write something positive about yourself or identify a skill that you have. If your name were Mara or Raul, it might look something like this:

Musical

Artistic

Responsible

Athletic

Runs for exercise

Apples for snacks

Upbeat personality

Logical

Being able to recognize your strengths and abilities provides you with courage to accept yourself. It helps you believe in yourself and what you want.

Some people recognize their strengths but believe they must do everything perfectly. If they don't, they may feel unhappy with themselves. They may decide to quit rather than make a mistake. This attitude is called perfectionism. If you feel that way, recognize that everyone makes mistakes. Without mistakes, people would never learn anything.

When you make mistakes, you may be getting the message that you need to slow down. Maybe you need to take a break or look at other options. Sometimes to move forward, it is helpful to consider the past. What have you tried that didn't work? What could you have done differently to make a situation more successful? How might that make a difference in the future?

ADVICE FROM TEENS

"There's a lot of stress being a teen today. The best advice I can give you is to get involved in this world that needs teens. I've joined a peer mediation group at school. It's helped me feel like I have a lot more control than I used to."–Tova, age 14

Making Sense of Your Life

You may be excited to learn about yourself. However, it can be a bit frightening if you discover you dislike some of your behaviors. You can change your behaviors and attitudes. For example, maybe you're not always polite to people. You have to decide if you want to be more polite. Then you need to decide how to do it.

Becoming self-directed may involve understanding how you fit into the world around you. You may see that what you say and do need to match. For example, you might believe people shouldn't make fun of others. If so, you should be ready to defend someone whom others make fun of.

Changing your behaviors to be more positive and to help others can give you a deep sense of accomplishment. When you have that sense, teachers, coaches, parents, employers, friends, and others often notice. You may feel a new respect from them.

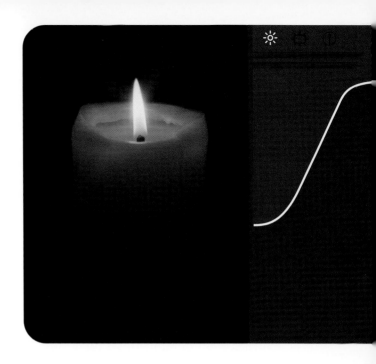

Think about this saying: "Blowing out the candles of others doesn't make your candle shine more brightly." Self-direction does not mean achieving recognition at the expense of others. The belief that people achieve success by putting others down is destructive. Perhaps a better attitude is to find a way everyone can win. One way is to use your talents and skills to help other people.

Ed, Age 15

Ed wanted to do volunteer work, but he wasn't sure what to do. Ed had helped his grandparents quite a bit until they died. Ed decided he wanted to keep helping older people. He asked his school counselor if she knew ways he could help. She suggested a meal delivery service for older people who couldn't get out of their house. Ed wasn't old enough to drive yet, but he could help an adult drop off the meals. Ed thought it was a good start.

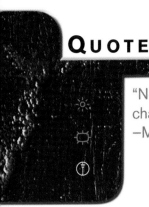

"Never doubt that a small, dedicated group of people can change the world. Indeed, it is the only thing that ever has."
—Margaret Mead, anthropologist

Making a Difference in Your Community

Self-direction often involves thinking about others. Your energy and confidence can be translated into action. For example, you may want your school to be safe and drug-free. You may want your friends to avoid self-destructive behaviors such as drinking. Here are some steps that can help you help others.

Choose a project that you are passionate about. Many teens can connect personal interests and enthusiasm with needs in their community.

1. Identify a goal. Is there a service project you might start? Some teen groups trick-or-treat for charities in October. Some teens tutor others in reading skills. Some teens deliver food and other gifts during holiday seasons. Your goal should be measurable. Imagine you want to collect toys for the holidays. Set a goal of a specific number of toys, which you will deliver on a specific date. Then you can see how well you do.

Maybe you want to propose a student policy regarding dress code. What are the facts? How do you feel? What will you say? Who will listen? What is the benefit to yourself and others? Start small if you have never organized a project. For example, maybe you decide on an antismoking campaign. You might want to begin by displaying posters in your neighborhood.

Self-Direction

You can ask some of these groups for support:

Private nonprofit groups: places of worship, Urban League, college groups such as fraternities or sororities, veterans' groups, National Association for the Advancement of Colored People (NAACP)

Business groups: chambers of commerce, corporate foundations

Professional groups: medical associations, social workers' associations, teachers' unions, and other unions

Volunteer organizations: Salvation Army, Goodwill, Rotary and Lions clubs, American Association of University Women

Community agencies: city and county social service agencies, mental health agencies, police departments, housing authority, school district, tribal councils, neighborhood associations, libraries, hospitals

Youth groups: Big Brothers/Big Sisters, Girl/Boy Scouts, Boys/Girls Club, YWCA, YMCA

2. Write a plan of action. Your plan should include tasks that each person should do. It also should include when things need to be done and how you might raise money. For example, if you want to put up posters, you might form a committee to call local printers. You might ask the printers to donate paper or print the posters for free.

3. Link up with similar groups. If other groups are doing similar work, join them or ask them to join you. There is strength in numbers.

4. Keep others informed. Send out press releases to local media. Find out how to submit public service announcements to TV and radio stations. Be sure to include information about how people can contact you for more information. Choose the most powerful facts to inform local leaders such as the city council about your issue.

5. Be trusting and committed to change. Decide how the project is going and learn from your mistakes. Don't give up easily, even if things seem to be going against you. Trust yourself and the people you are working with.

Self-Direction

Points to Consider: OtherMatters

Can a self-directed person be shy? Explain.

What are some ways a person can build confidence?

How important is it to expect that everyone you meet will like you? Why?

How is self-direction related to perfectionism?

Note

At publication, all resources listed here were accurate and appropriate to the topics covered in this book. Addresses and phone numbers may change. When visiting Internet sites and links, use good judgment.

Internet Sites

Canadian Health Network
www.canadian-health-network.ca
Links to health topics in Canada

Go Ask Alice!
www.goaskalice.columbia.edu/index.html
Factual, straightforward answers to teens'
questions about sexual, physical, emotional,
and spiritual health

Iwannaknow.org
www.iwannaknow.org
Information on teen sexual health

KidsHealth.Org for Teens
www.kidshealth.org/teen/index.html
Health information for teens

Teenwire
www.teenwire.com
Information on sex, life, and other teen issues

Useful Addresses

American Social Health Association
PO Box 13827
Research Triangle Park, NC 27709
www.ashastd.org

National Institute on Alcohol Abuse and
Alcoholism (NIAAA)
6000 Executive Boulevard
Willco Building
Bethesda, MD 20892-7003
www.niaaa.nih.gov

National Institute of Mental Health
6001 Executive Boulevard
Room 8184
MSC 9663
Bethesda, MD 20892-9663
www.nimh.nih.gov/research/suicide.htm

National Mental Health Association
1021 Prince Street
Alexandria, VA 22314-2971
www.nmha.org

Partnership for a Drug-Free America
405 Lexington Avenue, 16th Floor
New York, NY 10174
www.drugfreeamerica.org

Planned Parenthood Federation of America
810 Seventh Avenue
New York, NY 10019
www.plannedparenthood.org

Students Against Destructive Decisions
(SADD)
PO Box 800
Marlborough, MA 01752
www.saddonline.com

For Further Reading

Benson, Peter L., Pamela Espelund, and Judy Galbraith. *What Teens Need to Succeed: Proven, Practical Ways to Shape Your Own Future.* Minneapolis: Free Spirit, 1998.

Covey, Sean. *The Seven Habits of Highly Effective Teens.* New York: Simon and Schuster, 1998.

Folkers, Gladys, and Jeanne Engelmann. *Taking Charge of My Mind and Body: A Girls' Guide to Outsmarting Alcohol, Drug, Smoking, and Eating Problems.* Minneapolis: Free Spirit, 1997.

Ross, Patricia, and Jodi Owens-Kristenson. *Take Charge of Your Life!* Tinley Park, IL: Goodheart-Willcox, 1996.

Wandberg, Robert. *Resilience: Bouncing Off, Bouncing Back.* Mankato, MN: Capstone, 2001.

Glossary

advocate (AD-vuh-kate)—to argue for something or speak on someone's behalf

carcinogenic (car-sin-uh-JEN-ik)—able to cause cancer

chlamydia (kluh-MID-ee-uh)—most common sexually transmitted disease in the United States

chronic (KRON-ik)—long lasting

environment (en-VYE-ruhn-muhnt)—the surroundings in which a person lives

genetic (juh-NET-ik)—related to traits that are passed from parents to children

health (HELTH)—complete physical, mental and emotional, and social well-being

health care (HELTH KAIR)—places and people such as clinics, hospitals, and doctors; health care helps people remain or get healthy.

individualism (in-duh-VID-joo-wuhl-iz-uhm)—ability to follow one's own instincts despite pressure from others

interpersonal skills (in-tur-PUR-suh-nuhl SKILZ)—skills that allow people to get along well with each other

optimistic (op-tuh-MISS-tik)—able to see the positive side of an issue or challenge

premature death (PREE-muh-chur DETH)—death that occurs earlier than normally expected

resilience (ri-ZIL-yuhnss)—the ability to bounce back from disappointment or hardship

value (VAL-yoo)—a principle, standard, or quality that a person considers to be good or worthwhile

Index

advocacy, 47, 48. *See also* groups (community)
AIDS, 30
alcohol, 10, 11, 27, 56
Ali, Muhammad, 33, 39
Anderson, Marian, 33, 37
arsenic, 26
assertiveness, 44
attitude, 5, 15, 33, 44, 53, 54, 55

behaviors, 19, 25, 28, 47, 48, 54

career, 8, 10
Carver, George Washington, 33, 38
Centers for Disease Control and Prevention (CDC), 19, 27
change, 20, 45, 46, 54, 58
chlamydia, 29
choices, 9, 11, 27, 35, 36
  health, 13, 15, 28
  lifestyle, 27, 30
communication skills, 20, 45
community, 28, 46, 47, 56–58
confidence, 5, 44, 48, 56
conflict resolution skills, 46
consequences, 10–11
critical thinking skills, 47, 48
Cruise, Tom, 33, 41

death, premature, 24, 28
decisions, 6, 8, 10–11, 13, 54
diseases, 13, 16, 18, 19, 25, 26, 27, 29, 30, 40
drugs, 10, 11, 19, 27, 35

eating patterns, 10, 27
Edison, Thomas, 33, 37, 40
education, 8, 12, 13, 38, 40, 41
environment, 19, 23, 24, 25, 26
Estefan, Gloria, 33, 40
exercise, 10, 17, 19, 21, 27, 52

failure, 33, 36, 37, 40, 41
friendliness, 19, 44, 48
FutureMatters, 43

genetics, 23, 24–25, 26
goals, 5, 8, 9, 10, 11, 44, 45, 56
  and community projects, 56
  and health, 10–11, 16, 20
  and sexually transmitted diseases (STDs), 11, 13
  and skills, 48
  and teen pregnancy, 12
groups (community), 54, 56, 57. *See also* advocacy

health, 5, 9, 10–11, 14–21, 28, 45
  behaviors, 10–11
  choices, 15, 28
  circles representing, 18
  consequences, 10–11
  cultural differences, 16
  decisions, 10–11, 13
  defining, 15–18
  mental and emotional, 7, 15, 18, 20
  physical, 15, 17, 18, 19
  social, 15, 18, 20
health care, 16, 24, 26
HealthMatters, 15

Index Continued